The Yoga Mindset
Journal

The Yoga Mindset Journal

Change Your Mindset, Change Your Life

Michelle Gervais-Bryan

Published by Game Changer Publishing

Cover Design by Margaret Bryan, Graphic Designer,
https://www.behance.net/maggiebryandesigns
Mandala Illustration purchased at www.shutterstock.com

ISBN: 978-1-7370407-1-2

GC | Game Changer
PUBLISHING

www.PublishABestSellingBook.com

DEDICATION

Every so often, a very special person passes through this world who not only sees the best in everyone they meet, but also takes great joy in helping those people grow, advance, and live out their life purpose. This person operates from a place of divine love, expecting neither praise nor payback, and they are a gift to the world. This person is none other than my extraordinary husband, Dan. My love, thank you for showing me how to live, laugh and love so well, and for perpetually restoring my faith in both God and humanity by simply being you. You are my hero. This book is lovingly dedicated to you, first and foremost, and to a few other beautiful souls that I've been privileged to know, love, and learn from in this lifetime.

To my brave and beautiful mother, Carol, thank you for surviving, for keeping me, and for whispering into my eyes, ears, and heart that I am enough for anything I set my mind to doing.

To my brilliant sister, Alisa, thank you for being my first best little sis, playmate, and friend.

To my feisty great aunts, Emma and Caroline, thank you for helping me see God in everything.

To my crazy fun aunt, Sharon, thank you for loving the small broken things of the world.

To my faithful stepfather, KJ, thank you for caring for widows and orphans in their distress.

To my best friend, Tonya, thank you for opening your heart and home when I needed it most.

To my amazing children, Joseph, Maggie, and Samuel, the light of my eyes and the song in my heart. You are enough, and you, too, can do anything you set your mind to doing. I love you.

You've all taught me how to live the best version of myself and my life. I am eternally grateful.

DOWNLOAD YOUR FREE GIFTS

Read This First

Just to say thanks for buying and reading my journal, I would like to give you three bonus gifts for FREE, no strings attached!

To Download Now, Visit:
www.TheYogaMindsetJournal.com/JournalFreeGifts

The Yoga Mindset Journal

Change Your Mindset, Change Your Life

Michelle Gervais-Bryan

GC Game Changer
PUBLISHING

www.PublishABestSellingBook.com

I am not what happened to me,
I am what I choose to become.

Carl Jung

FOREWORD

"I saw the angel in the marble and carved until I set him free."
Michelangelo

In the summer of 2016, Michelle Gervais-Bryan presented me with a massive boulder, hewn from the caves of her life, along with a request to help her release the angel that was stuck inside.

I recognize a good story when I hear it, and this one hooked me immediately. It needed to be told, but I could see that she needed some guidance on how and where to begin.

With great care and precision, I guided her in the placement of both the mallet and the chisel, from one manuscript to the next, until all that needed to be subtracted was removed and only the essence of what was necessary remained. With the final blow of the mallet, we both stepped back and marveled at the breathtaking masterpiece that was always there, just below the surface. That same sense of breakthrough to the best version of your life awaits in the pages of this book.

We are all in this thing called 'life' together, and though it's not always easy, there are three timeless secrets that can make it a masterpiece. *The Yoga Mindset* is the key to unlocking those secrets, and Michelle is your guide each step of the way.

With the wonder of a child, the eye of an artist and the precision of a sculptor, she will guide you in the placement of both the mallet and the chisel on the rock of *your* life, until all that needs to be subtracted is removed, and only the essence of what is necessary, and a masterpiece, remains, too.

With whole-hearted enthusiasm, I recommend this book to anyone who knows, deep down inside, that they were meant for so much more, and are ready to begin the journey to true freedom.

Samuel H. Bryan, Founder & Editor
The Red Cellar Door Collective

Table of Contents

INTRODUCTION

There is an ancient Japanese legend that tells the story of a mighty shogun warrior who broke his favorite tea bowl and sent it away for repairs. When it was returned to him, and he saw the unsightly staples holding the broken pieces together, he was displeased. Hoping to restore it to its former beauty, he sent it out to a craftsman with a request for a more elegant solution.

The craftsman knew exactly what to do. He used a new repair technique that would not only restore the bowl to its original beauty but also increase its value. He carefully joined all the broken pieces back together with a lacquer resin mixed with precious gold. When it was returned to the warrior, and he saw the streaks of gold running throughout the bowl telling its story, he was pleased.

This new method of repair became known as *kintsugi* or "golden joinery." It expressed the Japanese philosophy of ascribing great value to things, not based on their perfection but on their imperfection.

This simple, but profound, story reminds me that, to one degree or another, we are all *kintsugi*. Some of us are like the bowl before the start of the story, not yet 'impacted' by the world. Others are like the broken bowl, feeling shattered into a thousand fragments, as a result of some life experience. Some are in the process of mending those fragments with lines of gold. Others, restored and feeling whole again, have returned to fulfilling their purpose in life as perfectly imperfect vessels.

Of all the possible *kintsugi* stages, where would you say *you* are at this moment in your life? What's your kintsugi story?

My *kintsugi* story begins one degree north of the equator in tropical Singapore. My family and I had just been transferred there after several years of living and working in Japan, and we were in the chaotic throes of unpacking and setting up our new home. Singapore's hot and balmy temperatures were both a shock to the system and a mirror image of the hot mess I felt like on the inside. Not quite ready to deal with all of my own 'personal baggage,' I instead found a job and started working. I was offered a position with a Singaporean architectural design studio, and I was completely and happily distracted from all of my deeper issues. I was living the expat life and loving it, but deep down, I knew that I was restless in my spirit. I knew that I would eventually need to take a deep dive into all of it, but I didn't really know where, or how to begin, and I surely didn't have the time since I was now so busy working. Singapore would eventually show me the way.

At 6 am, before the hustle and bustle of the emerald city begins, a committed group of expats and Singaporeans gather on the second floor of a dimly lit row house in Chinatown that has been converted into a hot yoga studio. With an outdoor temperature of 87 degrees and what feels like 100 percent humidity, plus an intentionally-set indoor temperature of 105 degrees. The studio is a steamy example of British architecture during the roaring 20s with soaring ceilings, at least twenty feet high, punctuated by a couple of lazy palm leaf-shaped ceiling fans. The windows are equally tall and open to the street below. The sheer white curtains shimmer as the fans leisurely sift the rising hot air back down towards the floor and the sweltering participants.

The thin black yoga mats are aligned so tightly that they are almost touching on all four sides, and most everyone is sitting, or lying down, on their mats, trying to acclimate to the heat and the negligible personal space. Most eyes are closed, and words are spoken in hushed tones. The collective breath moves slowly and deeply.

The light in the room is minimal at best since the sun has not yet risen, but in the semi-darkness, I spy an open mat at the back of the room. "Thank God it's in the back," I think to myself, and I walk over to settle in. I'd taken and taught traditional yoga classes, but this was my first 'hot' yoga class. My neighbor, also a new expat in Singapore, invited me, explaining that it would be life-altering. As a fitness instructor and personal trainer, I was definitely interested, but I didn't really buy into the whole life-altering bit. Nonetheless, I was new to the area and feeling ready to connect, so I accepted the offer.

As I was sitting completely still on my mat, beads of sweat started rolling down my spine. A slight discomfort set in, and I began to wonder about the wisdom of my decision. I'd suffered from panic attacks for several years, for reasons I still couldn't explain, and the setting was not exactly ideal for someone prone to panic attacks. I was starting to feel some anxiety rising.

"Not again," I sighed to myself. I started talking myself down from the ledge. "Breathe, you are safe. Look around. No one is harming you. It's just hot as Hades," I told myself. My anxiety was still rising. "Maybe I just needed a fresh breath of air," I thought to myself. Gazing over my shoulder at the door behind me, I got up and slipped out quickly. In the open space of the lobby, I inhaled the cool air deeply, exhaled and relaxed. Then I reminded myself again that all was well and that I could walk out again, at any time, if I wanted, or needed, to do so. That did the trick. Feeling the anxiety subside, my heart rate slowed, and I stepped back into the sauna. Everything was exactly as I left it, except for the new and subtle smell of sweat and perspiration now weaving itself into the air.

Like standing in the foam at the edge of the ocean, the deep and focused breathing created a soft wave of sound all around me. Gently breaking through the surf, in an enchanting accent that was not quite English and not quite Singaporean, the Yoga Instructor calmly greeted everyone, introduced himself as our guide, and invited us to stand together to begin. With our hands to our hearts in prayer position, we inhaled, exhaled, and, like the ocean, we began to flow.

For one hour, the instructor guided us through a series of synchronized poses and breathwork, peppered with moments of stillness and contemplation. There wasn't any music, only his voice, rising and falling like the waves of the ocean, urging everyone to find the fullest expression in each of the poses: to reach a little farther, to root a little deeper, and to exhale a little more expansively amidst the now rising waves of ocean breathing.

At some point, I lost track of the edges of myself in relation to the others. It felt like we were all one giant ocean wave moving together in a series of massive ebbs and flows of both breath and presence. We reached up, we folded forward, we swayed, we twisted, we opened our hearts, we closed our eyes, we inhaled, we exhaled, we focused, we balanced, we inverted, we extended, we soared. It felt like a choreographed routine on Broadway that we all somehow knew by heart.

As we neared the end of the hour, we held the final pinnacle pose. As if I'd just finished a marathon, I was exhausted, exhilarated, and drenched. To slow my breathing and steady myself, I recovered my focal point in the distance and took a slow deep breath. I felt another thick bead of sweat run from my temple down my cheek in what seemed like slow motion. As that bead of sweat fell from my chin to the floor, I exhaled, and time slowed to a crawl.

The high tide of ocean breath in the room receded to a whisper, and I felt like I was floating somewhere between the earth and the sky, a kite without a string, hovering, looking at everyone and everything below me. Time was meaningless. There was just the sensation of stillness in my body, the breathlessness in my lungs, and the vibration of my heart pumping blood throughout my body. I was aware of the people in the room, the sounds of the street below us, the city, the world, and the feeling of connectedness to all of it, all at once. The sun was rising and filtering in through the windows of the studio, illuminating everyone and everything.

After feeling so fragmented and lost to myself for so long, and for so many reasons, in the light of that moment, I was able to see the pieces of my life in a completely new way. I finally understood how they all fit together, and I saw them telling their story in beautiful lines of gold. It was a breathtaking mosaic of my life, a perfectly imperfect masterpiece, and it was beautiful. I smiled as a deep and much-needed rest washed over me, and I came out of Dancer Pose.

The yoga class came to an end and the instructor closed the practice. With our hands to our hearts once more, I bowed my head and my heart, full of more love, peace, and joy than I ever thought possible.

Feeling free from being perpetually stuck in the past, present and future, I was present and connected to myself and others, for the first time in a long time. It was as if my spirit, split three ways between the past, present and future, finally caught up with my body all at the same time. Not quite touching the ground, I floated out of that studio, thanked my friend for the invitation and confirmed that "*yes*, it was everything you said it would be and more." In fact, it was so life-altering that I never suffered another panic attack again.

Life continued to slam into me, a continuous and guaranteed hazard of being alive and in this world, but instead of being completely shattered by each new impact, I started to think of them as unanticipated upgrades and personal growth opportunities. Instead of complaining about the storm, I chose to look for the positive lessons so that I could get through it as quickly as possible. Instead of fighting against the winds of the storm, I chose to reposition my sail and harness the force of the winds to propel me forward to my chosen destination. I chose to flow with things as they were. I wish I could say that I have flowed perfectly in the face of every challenge, but that would not be true. I'm still human.

I still get upset. I still wonder why things happen the way they do. I'm still careless with my words and actions. I'm still a work in progress. Practice makes progress, and I'm getting better at flowing with life 'as it is' and progressing all the time.

The difference now is my mindset. Where I used to be a steamy hot mess unwilling to flow with things as they were, I have a constant, deep peace and calm. It's a peace that passes all understanding, and it sustains me when nothing else makes sense. It's far beyond the reach of any storm that I may face. It's far beyond the reach of this world or human thinking. My circumstances didn't change, but my thinking did.

That shift in thinking, that new mindset, what I call The Yoga Mindset, was a game changer. It helped me to see that what felt like life happening *to* me all the time was also life happening *for* me. Don't get me wrong. The storms of life were still devastating. I don't mean to minimize the reality of evil, pain and suffering in the world. It is very real and often tragic. Along those lines, if you ever find yourself in a situation where someone is dangerous to you, or others, please seek professional help and protection immediately.

Though we can't always control the circumstances of our lives, we always have a choice as to our response and the stories we tell ourselves about those challenges. They can be disempowering and keep us stuck in the past, or a dangerous and dysfunctional situation, or they can be empowering and liberate us to move forward to our best self and our best life. Which would you prefer? It's really all up to you. It's all in your mindset.

I've carried this gift of *The Yoga Mindset* for several years now, and it has made all the difference in my life. My hope is that it might be a game changer for you, too, but where to begin?

Like my dear friend, who invited me to that yoga class in Singapore, I would propose we start with a yoga class and The Yoga Mindset Formula. Join me for a yoga class in the pages of this Yoga Mindset Journal to hit the reset button on your body and your life.

No, you don't have to be super flexible or do pretzel yoga to get the full benefit of this journal. You just need a flexible mind, open to learning and practicing the seven secret alignment principles of one of the most fundamental poses in almost every yoga class: Mountain Pose. Additionally, you'll need to be open to applying those seven alignment principles to the seven related areas of your life through the chakras, an ancient health and wellness system that is still in use today.

I don't pretend to be an expert of the chakras, but I invite you to learn about them and use them as a guide to help you begin or go deeper into your practice and/or your life.

The seven chakras or key areas of the body and the mind that we'll focus on include:

1. The Feet and Legs: Your relationships with your family of origin or other tribe in your life including a sports group, a church group, a yoga group, etc.

2. Your Pelvis: Your relationships with other people outside your family of origin
3. The Core: Your relationship with yourself
4. The Heart: Your ability to give and receive love
5. The Throat: Your ability to speak and be heard
6. The Eyes: Your ability to see and be seen
7. The Crown of your Head: Your ability to know and be known by the Creator of everything. Some refer to the Creator of everything as God, Nature, Source, and various other names. For the purposes of this book, based on my faith, I will refer to the Creator as God.

This book is the companion journal to *The Yoga Mindset* book that goes into much greater detail about harnessing the power of the storms in our lives to rewire our brains for a better future. Whether you use this journal as a companion to the main book or on its own, you have the option to make it a seven-day challenge, a seven-week challenge, a seven-month challenge, or really any timeline of your choosing. All approaches are okay. Everyone's experience will be unique, so you decide the timeline that best serves you. We'll all meet at the top of the mountain eventually, and the view may be life-altering for you, too.

For this journey, you will be traveling light. You'll need this journal, a pen or pencil, a yoga mat, a designated space to practice, and courage to take a compassionate deep dive into your life.

If at any time on this journey, you find anything too challenging to address independently, for any reason whatsoever, it is recommended to talk with a trusted family member or friend. If that is not possible, it is strongly recommended to seek the help of a professional therapist or doctor who might be able to address any deeper issues.

At each of the seven stops along the trek, from the bottom to the top of this 'mountain', you'll consider the state of health of seven key areas of your life. Wherever you may feel 'stuck' along the path, or those seven areas, you'll be invited to look at the situation in a new way and then to flip the script on any disempowering stories you may have been telling yourself about those experiences that have kept you feeling stuck in life. You'll be encouraged to search for the lesson in each situation to help you start telling yourself new and empowering stories, woven together with lines of precious gold for a better future.

Set out everything that you'll need the night before. Read the chapter the day or night before, as well. Read all the questions for that chapter. You'll only have time to answer a few in five minutes, but you can always come back to the other questions later.

When you wake up, everything will be ready to go. Once in your space, set your timer for 15 minutes, or three five-minute increments, and get ready to move, meditate, and manifest your future as you define it!

That is your daily practice for seven days. Figure out what works best for you as far as timers and time of day. However you slice it, the shortest path to the top of this mountain is one chapter a day over seven days. To get the most out of this challenge, try to treat this time as sacred and aim to disconnect from technology for those 15 minutes to the greatest extent possible. For the first five minutes every morning, the first thing we'll do is move.

Why Move? — We move because our amazing bodies were designed to move and breathe daily. It's still the best medicine for everybody with manifold positive side effects. Set aside five minutes every morning to stand and breathe. Can't stand? No worries. You can do this sitting. Can't sit? It can be done lying down, as well. It's all in your mindset.

As far as when to practice, the first thing in the morning, before your day begins, is recommended. It's the golden window of opportunity when the noise of the day has not yet begun and you can set the tone and focus of your whole day, but if that is not an option, any other time of the day will do.

Trouble getting out of bed? I heartily recommend Mel Robbins' clever launching trick. When your alarm goes off, count backwards 5...4...3...2...1... and then, visualize yourself as a rocket, lifting off of a launchpad. Then do it. Get out of bed and begin to move. Once you are done with the move segment of the Yoga Mindset Formula, we'll meditate for the next five minutes.

Why Meditate? — This is the fruit of your movement, and it is the powerhouse of the Yoga Mindset Formula. As Anatomy Trains author, Thomas Meyers, declares, "Exercise from below helps us up above." We meditate after we move because it's the next step in the process of the mind-body connection. Meditation is focused thinking on something, like an inspirational quote, an object in the distance, or your breath. It's a way to calm a scattered mind to 'see' more clearly. Next, we'll manifest the best version of ourselves and our lives.

Why Manifest? — This is the fruit of your meditation. This is the part of the formula where you will proactively visualize, and co-create, the best version of yourself and your life by tapping into the ultimate power source, the Creator of everything.

I was raised in the Christian faith, so I refer to the Creator as the Christian God in this book. Some people refer to God as something different: Source, Creator, the Universe, and many other names. Whatever name you use, these last five minutes of the Yoga Mindset Formula have the potential to change the entire trajectory of your life as you plug into the ultimate power source, so give yourself permission to dream BIG!

You are the author of your life story, and you have the power to write, rewrite, and completely flip the script on any disempowering stories you may have been telling yourself about your life up to this point. I'm talking about flipping the script on the kind of stories that keep you stuck in pain and suffering long after an event occurred. If you can relate to feeling stuck and you are ready to start telling yourself new, better, and empowering stories, let's begin.

It's a great day to hit the reset button on your life. It's a great day to start living your life to the fullest, as a perfectly imperfect vessel, no matter your circumstances. It's all in your mindset.

You are here for a reason, and you have a purpose to fulfill in the short amount of time you've been given. Is there anything more important?

CHAPTER 1

I Am

"I should like to ask you:
Does your childhood seem far off?
Do the days when you sat at your mother's knee seem
days of very long ago?
Twenty years back, yes; at this time of my life, no.
For as I draw closer and closer to the end,
I travel in the circle, nearer and nearer to the beginning.
It seems to be one of kind smoothings and preparings of the way..."

Charles Dickens, *A Tale of Two Cities*

How and where did it all begin for you? What was it like in your family of origin? Were there things that were difficult? Were there things that were wonderful? What stories have you been telling yourself about those experiences all these years? Do those stories entrap you or empower you to move forward in life?

Let's look a little closer. Imagine that you are a building inspector and you've been assigned the job of inspecting the foundation of your life. You are looking for cracks, misalignment, and fragments; anything that would not support the structure of your life. No judgment required. I'm simply asking you to imagine that you are an unbiased observer. Just inspect and notice the state of the foundation supporting your life. Is it level, or cracked and off-center at certain points? Are there any dysfunctional patterns in your life? Any chance they are related to your family of origin?

In the same way that our family of origin, or our foundation, can affect the structure of our lives, our physical bodies can also be misaligned and dysfunctional. Practicing the first alignment principle of Mountain Pose will not only help to minimize those physical misalignments, but also help you flip the script on any negative stories you may have been telling yourself about your family of origin.

Mountain Pose is truly the foundation to all yoga poses and it all starts with the feet. You might be thinking, 'the feet?' Yes, the feet. In the same way that we take time to build the correct type of foundation beneath a massive structure, we need to also take time to consider what we do with the feet in Mountain Pose.

So, grab your timer, and let's set up both our mind and our bodies for success on this journey by establishing a solid foundation beneath us in Mountain Pose.

The Yoga Mindset Formula, Day 1

MOVE

Mountain Pose Alignment Principle #1: Set the Foundation

Set your timer for five minutes and move!

The Feet

1. Remove your socks and shoes, if possible. If not possible, exercise shoes are okay.
2. Stand with your feet about hip-width apart and parallel to each other on your mat.
3. Check to make sure that the 2nd and 3rd toes of both feet are in line with the heels.
4. Press the big toes, little toes, right edges of both heels, and left edges of both heels into the ground.

The Legs

1. With feet grounded, move the shins forward slightly, bending the knee.
2. Now, reverse it, but don't lock the knees.
3. Contract, or activate, the calf and thigh muscles to straighten the legs up.
4. Add just the right amount of a micro-bend in the knees.

5. Stand tall and feel the strength of your legs helping you reach up and the strength of your feet helping you press down, grounding towards the earth.

Breathwork

With your feet and legs firmly rooted in Mountain Pose, next let's breathe. Inhale and exhale for five to six slow counts for each breath below. If five to six counts for a breath makes you feel a bit claustrophobic, start with three to four slow breaths and eventually work your way up.

1. As you inhale and exhale slowly, visualize yourself as a tree. Imagine your roots shooting deep into the ground beneath you. See yourself grounded, supported, nourished by the earth, and growing strong, tall, and resilient.
2. As you inhale and exhale this second breath, visualize yourself firmly grounded and declare: 'I am' and 'I have a right to be here.'
3. As you take this last breath, stand firm, and rise up even higher, declaring that,"life is not happening *to* me, life is happening *for* me."
4. Repeat steps 1-3, as time permits.

When you have completed your five minutes of breathwork, remember to ground your feet wherever you are this week - at home, in the grocery store, in a meeting, at school or at work. Stand tall, and remind yourself that you are, simply because you exist, and then remind yourself that you have the right to be fully present wherever you are. Let's move on to mediation.

MEDITATE

Set your timer for five more minutes and prepare to meditate on the questions below. Answer questions six and seven below. Come back later to finish the other questions, if interested, and as time permits.

1. Who raised you?

2. Did you feel that the basic needs to be loved, supported, and protected in your family were met? Why or why not?

3. Do you know anything about your parents, or guardians, family of origin that may help explain why those basic needs were or were not met?

4. If these needs were not met, how did/does that play out in your life?

5. Are those patterns serving you in your family relationships? Why or why not?

6. Write out one to three negative experiences from your childhood, and then next to each one, write at least one positive result.

7. Flip the script on the disempowering stories you may have been telling yourself for years and write a new empowering story about each of your negative childhood experiences.

While we can't control all the circumstances of our lives, we can always choose our responses. You can choose to stay stuck in the past, in unforgiveness, for yourself or someone else, or you can choose to see how it was actually working for you, you can find the lessons, and then use that insight to flip the script on the stories you've been telling yourself about those life challenges. It's time to find a way to move forward towards the best version of yourself and your life?

MANIFEST

Set your timer for five more minutes. Consider how you can 'show up' differently within your family of origin moving forward, as a result of your new insight and empowered stories.

Take some time to journal about how you might be able to 'show up' differently in your family of origin, or any of your 'tribes', moving forward, and as a result of the new stories you choose to tell yourself. Keep in mind that showing up doesn't necessarily mean in person. It could be from a distance, if the situation is unsafe for you or anyone else. Whether in person, or from a safe distance, how can you show up differently for yourself, your family, or any other of your tribes?

PRACTICE

The Yoga Mindset Formula in REAL TIME

Today, or anytime, before stepping into a difficult family situation, or whenever you unexpectedly find yourself in a difficult family situation, practice the Yoga Mindset Formula.

1. **MOVE:** Inhale for five to six slow counts and exhale for five to six slow counts as you stand with your feet hip width apart and firmly planted in Mountain Pose.

2. **MEDITATE:** Declare, "Life is not happening *to* me, life is happening *for* me."

3. **MANIFEST:** Visualize yourself firmly rooted, supported, and grounded and remind yourself of your new insights on the lessons from any negative experiences with your family of origin. Act on your intention to 'show up' differently within your family, or tribe, based on the new and empowering stories you choose to tell yourself.

The Yoga Mindset Principle #1:
I am, and I have the right to be here.
The Yoga Mindset Mantra:
Life is not happening *to* me, life is happening *for* me.

CHAPTER 2

I Feel

"I crave your mouth, your voice, your hair/
Silent and starving, I prowl through the streets/
Bread does not nourish me, dawn disrupts me/
All day I hunt for the liquid measure of your steps."

Pablo Neruda, *Love Sonnet XI*

In a Ted Talk by Katie Hood, she wondered aloud, "Isn't it interesting that we've never actually been taught how to love? The truth is that we often harm and disrespect the ones we love. One hundred percent of us will be on the receiving end of unhealthy behaviors, and one hundred percent of us will do unhealthy things. It's part of being human. In its worst form, the harm we inflict on others shows up as abuse and violence. The truth is that unhealthy relationships are all around us. Pay attention to how your relationship grows." Great advice! If only I'd heard it when I was younger.

Around the age of 18, I wasn't paying too much attention to how my first deeply intimate relationship had been growing. There were many red flags, but I didn't want to see them because I was in 'love.' As a result, I walked in on my boyfriend, Jake, in bed with another woman just a few months into our relationship. Devastated doesn't even begin to describe how I struggled after that soul-crushing moment.

As devastating as it was, it was exactly the thing that needed to happen in order for me to move forward. Life was happening for me, but I had to choose to look for the positive lessons. Then, I had to flip the script in my mind. Had that painful moment never happened, I wouldn't have found the path to my greatest life blessings: my now husband, soulmate and best friend and my children and my life now. All along, life was not happening *to* me, life was happening *for* me.

In the same way that I was able to recover the balance in myself with time, we must often do the same with our physical body from time to time. In this chapter, we'll focus on the pelvis. This part of the body houses our reproductive organs and relates to our sexuality, creativity and intimate relationships, so let's start by bringing the pelvis to a neutral position (not too far back or forward) for more balanced physical health and, applying that concept a bit further to our lives, for more balanced intimate relationships.

The Yoga Mindset Formula, Day 2

MOVE

Mountain Pose Alignment Principle #2: Bring the Pelvis to Neutral

Set your timer for five minutes and move!

The Pelvis

1. Stand with your feet about hip-width apart. Ensure that the 2nd and 3rd toes are in line with heels and that the four corners of your feet (big toes, little toes, and both sides of the heels) are pressing down firmly on the ground. Stack your knees over your ankles and your hips over the knees. Move your shins forward and pull your thighs back. Stand tall with calves and thighs contracted and active while keeping that barely-perceptible micro-bend in the knee.
2. Now, shift your hips, also referred to as the pelvis, to a neutral position between the two extremes of too far forward and too far back by contracting the abdominal muscles and tucking the tailbone down gently towards the floor while still maintaining the natural S curve of your lower back.
3. Pull the rib cage back slightly and then stand tall by lifting your heart.

Scan your body. How does this neutral hip position feel? If you sit a lot during the day, or if you stand with a pronounced arch in your lower back, it may feel a little unusual, but a balanced neutral position of the hips, still maintaining the natural S curve of the lower back, can relieve a lot of pressure on the back and help to strengthen the abdominal and back muscles over time.

Expanding that thought a bit further to our lives, you can also shift your more intimate relationships back to a more neutral, balanced, and healthy place if they have been to one extreme or the other. As you practice this pelvis alignment each day, remind yourself that you have the ability to enjoy both healthy and balanced physical alignment and healthy and balanced intimate relationships.

Breathwork

Keep moving with the breath. Inhale slowly for five to six counts and exhale slowly for five to six counts for each breathing exercise below.

1. Standing with your feet hip width apart in Mountain Pose, imagine yourself as a tree. Imagine your roots shooting deep into the ground beneath you. Imagine yourself anchored, strong, and resilient, flowing, forward and back, with the wind, but not breaking.

2. In that grounded stance, shift your hips to a neutral position and remind yourself that you can enjoy both healthy and balanced physical alignment and healthy and balanced intimate relationships.

3. Maintaining that neutral pelvis, declare to yourself that "Life is not happening *to* me, life is happening *for* me."

Think of applying those subtle adjustments to your pelvis and your relationships everyday moving forward. At first, the changes might not be noticeable, but over time you may start to perceive the benefits in decreased back pain, increased core strength and more balanced intimate relationships.

MEDITATE

Set your timer for five minutes and meditate. Answer questions one and three below. Come back to answer the remaining questions, if interested, and as time permits.

1. Can you list one to three difficult intimate relationships that you've experienced in the past, or are currently experiencing, and journal a bit about what happened, or is happening?

2. For each negative experience listed, why do you think they were, or are, difficult?

3. For each negative relationship experience listed in question one, look for ways it might be working for you. List the lesson learned, and journal about how that might actually be able to help you to move forward in your life and in your intimate relationships.

4. What steps are needed on your part to change or improve the quality of your intimate relationships moving forward?

5. How can you start moving forward towards healthier and more balanced relationships in your life? Write out and prioritize the steps you need to take and take action!

MANIFEST

Set your timer for five more minutes, and journal about how you might be able to 'show up' differently in your intimate relationships moving forward based on the lessons learned. Flip the script on any negative and disempowering stories you may have been telling yourself about yourself and your intimate relationships and create new and empowering stories to help yourself move forward.

Remember that showing up doesn't necessarily mean in person. It could be from a distance if the situation is unsafe for you or anyone else. In person, or from a safe distance, how can you show up differently? It could be a new way of thinking about someone, a text, a phone call, a letter, a request to a loved one about how you can love them better, or some other act of appreciation or service. It's all up to you. Your relationships may not change, but you can.

PRACTICE

The Yoga Mindset in REAL TIME:

Today, or anytime, if you wish to improve your intimate relationships beyond your family of origin, practice the Yoga Mindset in real time!

1. **MOVE:** Stand in Mountain Pose and inhale slowly for five to six counts and exhale slowly for five to six counts.
2. **MEDITATE:** Declare that "Life is not happening *to* me, life is happening *for* me."
3. **MANIFEST:** Visualize yourself in healthy and balanced relationships, and then act on your intention to take the steps needed to create healthier intimate relationships in person, or from a distance, if necessary.

The Yoga Mindset Principle #2
I have the right to feel both emotionally and physically.
The Yoga Mindset Mantra
Life is not happening *to* me, life is happening *for* me.

CHAPTER 3

I Do

"Our deepest fear is not that we are inadequate.
Our deepest fear is that we are powerful beyond measure.
It is our light, not our darkness, that most frightens us.
We ask ourselves, 'Who am I to be brilliant, gorgeous,
talented, fabulous?'
Actually, who are you not to be?"

Marianne Williamson

In the fall of 1985, I applied to the School of Architecture & Urban Design at Virginia Tech. I loved every brain-altering minute of that introductory intensive summer program, and I felt like I had finally recovered the core of who I was after a very difficult relationship. I also felt like I'd found my place and my tribe. Joy was seeping back into my life. I was smiling a little wider, standing a little taller and finally moving forward in my life again.

Speaking of standing tall, have you ever noticed that a lot of people are hunched over a phone or a computer these days? Others may have that same hunched posture because they feel like they've lived the majority of their lives defeated or devastated by one too many hard knocks. As a result, the core of who they are, as well as their actual physical core, can become weak. It's a recipe for injury and pain. Sound familiar? If you can relate, and honestly, I suspect most of us can relate at one point or another in our lives, the next step in Mountain Pose, 'sealing the core,' can help. Take your time with this one.

Give yourself permission to reconnect with the core of who you are. Close your eyes and remember the essence of who you are. Then, imagine someone putting a corset around your body and pulling the strings tightly. Can you imagine how the core might 'seal' tight on all sides when the strings are cinched? Keeping the core sealed tight, next, roll your shoulders back and down and think of lifting your heart up as you stand tall again. If it's been a while since you've sealed your core and stood tall, take it slowly and simply notice how you feel in this empowering stance. Whether sitting or standing during your day, practice sealing the core and lifting your heart. Give yourself permission to plant your feet firmly on the ground, to activate your legs, to bring your pelvis to neutral, to seal your core, and to lift your heart. Strengthen the core of who you are with this alignment principle and by doing things that grow your confidence. Set and accomplish your personal goals. These small incremental personal and physical adjustments can help increase your confidence, and that is often reflected in your posture, which speaks volumes to those around you.

The Yoga Mindset Formula, Day 3

MOVE

Mountain Pose Alignment Principle #3: Seal the Core

Set your timer for five minutes and move!

The Abdominal Muscles

1. Set your foundation with your feet rooted firmly into the ground, about hip-width apart, 2nd and 3rd toes in line with the heels, shins forward, thighs back, legs strong, and standing tall. Add that knee-saving microbend, rock the pelvis forward and back and then find that healthy and balanced neutral position for the pelvis, and let's seal the core.

2. Measure about three to four fingers below the belly button. This is the focal point of our contraction. From deep inside, as if you were trying to stop the flow of your urine in the bathroom, contract the muscles of the pelvic floor.

3. Keeping the deep pelvic floor muscles tight, now contract the lower abdominal muscles towards that focal point, then slightly up towards your heart. You should feel tight below your belly button right now, almost as if someone has just tightly wrapped your lower abdomen and lower back with a corset or plastic wrap.

Ribs & Sides of the Body

1. Holding the contraction in your lower abdominals, next start to lift your heart and the sides of your body up (often referred to as the 'side bodies' in yoga) while shifting the rib cage back slightly.
2. Stack your spine directly over the neutral pelvis. How does this feel? It may feel a bit unusual if you've not stood tall for a while.
3. Find that balanced, aligned, and neutral spine and pelvic position. Find the place where you are strong, but not stiff; open, but not overly relaxed.

Breathwork

Inhale slowly for five to six counts and exhale slowly for five to six counts for each breath below.

1. Standing in Mountain Pose, visualize yourself as a palm tree near the ocean. Imagine it is bending over with the winds from a tropical storm, strong and resilient. See it as flowing with the force of the storms in your life, but not uprooted or devastated by it.
2. In that grounded stance, seal your core, lift your heart, and remind yourself that you have the right to reconnect with the core of who you are and to set and achieve goals.
3. With your heart lifted up and your core sealed, declare that "Life is not happening *to* me, life is happening *for* me."

When done, if time permits, continue with your breathwork. Aim to maintain those subtle adjustments to your core and your relationship with yourself regarding setting and accomplishing your goals throughout your day. At first, the changes might not be noticeable, but over time you can start to perceive the benefits and may also start to smile a little wider and stand a little taller.

In the next segment of the Yoga Mindset Formula, you will practice giving yourself permission to dream, to set goals, and to achieve them. I'm going to ask you to be a bit selfish, to achieve all you envision for yourself in your life.

MEDITATE

Set your timer for five minutes. Answer questions three and four and come back later to answer the other questions, if interested, and as time permits.

1. List three things you'd like to change about yourself, and then list three things you like about yourself.

2. Was it easier to rattle off the negative and harder to think of the positive? Why do you think that is?

3. Can you list one to three experiences in your life that negatively impacted your self-confidence?

4. What are the positive lessons in those negative experiences that you listed in question number three?

5. Just for a moment, imagine...if money were no object and the sky was the limit, what would you want your life to look like? For yourself - your health, your physical body, your mind, your self-confidence? What would your family, friends, intimate relationships, and your professional, spiritual, and financial relationships look like? What about your retirement years and your legacy to your family or the world? Close your eyes and visualize it and then write about it.

6. Coming back to the present moment, for each category listed in question five, what will you do first? Second? Third? Write it out below, then list the steps you can take in order to increase the chances of that overall vision eventually becoming a reality.

7. Where can you begin today to start moving forward towards your number one goal above? Create an action plan and then move. Do the same for the other goals. Take action to create a better life for yourself!

MANIFEST

Set your timer for five minutes and manifest the best version of your life. Journal about how you might be able to 'show up' differently with regard to your self-confidence, your dreams, and your life goals moving forward based on the lessons you've gleaned from your negative experiences.

Perhaps a first step could be a goal to daily practice physically sealing your core for a week. It could be making a vision board of all the things you want to manifest for yourself in the current year. It's really all up to you. While you can't control all the circumstances of your life, that may have negatively impacted your self-confidence, at any time, you can choose to see the lessons in the challenges and then reframe your response. You can tell yourself new and better stories. Those new and improved thoughts, that new mindset, can then assist you in recovering and reconnecting to the core of who you are. Perhaps, in time you too may smile a little wider, stand a bit taller, dream a little bigger, set big goals again, and do the work of achieving, too. Let's get those thoughts down on paper.

1. Make a list of all the things you want for yourself. The things you REALLY dream for yourself. If you could wave a wand over your life what you wish for: physically, mentally, emotionally, intellectually, relationally, professionally, financially, spiritually. This is the part of the book where I'm going to ask you to dream BIG! Just for a moment, imagine that anything was possible. What would you want for yourself and your life in each category?

2. Based on your list in question number one, now make a list of the realistic and specific steps that would need to occur in order for you to start moving in the direction of the best version of yourself and your life in each category. Mark each item off as it manifests in your life. Look at and think on these goals daily and watch for the opportunities, people, and resources that may start to appear in your life in order to support you on your journey.

PRACTICE

The Yoga Mindset in REAL TIME:

Today, or anytime you feel your self-confidence waning, or you want to set and accomplish some personal goals, apply the Yoga Mindset steps below in real time!

1. **MOVE:** Stand in Mountain Pose with your core sealed and heart lifted. Inhale slowly for five to six counts and exhale slowly for five to six counts.
2. **MEDITATE:** Declare: "Life is not happening *to* me, life is happening *for* me."
3. **MANIFEST:** Visualize yourself as a healthy, competent, and confident person, standing firm and tall, setting goals and crushing them, even if it takes several attempts to cross them off your lifts, moving forward in life, like a magnificent tree soaring up towards the sky. Then act on your intention to move forward in strengthening the core of who you are and in building your self-confidence as you do the work of setting and achieving your personal goals.

Yoga Mindset Principle #3:
I have the right to set and achieve my goals.
The Yoga Mindset Mantra:
Life is not happening *to* me, it's happening *for* me.

CHAPTER 4

I Love

"Please call me by my true name
so I can wake up,
and so the door of my heart can be left open,
the door of compassion."

Thich Nhat Hanh

As strange as it sounds, my father's untimely death, the challenges of my parent's marriage, my stepfather's emotional absence after the loss of his daughter, my mother's struggles with mental health, and my difficult relationship with Jake all needed to happen exactly as it did for me to be where I am today. I couldn't say any of that when those circumstances were occurring. I could barely even function when it was happening. It was awful. I would have laughed, or possibly screamed, at anyone who told me to trust that all of it was working *for* me. Now, however, I can see more clearly. I see how it was all working together to create the best possible version of myself and my life.

While you will never be able to control people or the circumstances that reliably slam into your life, you can choose to find the positive lessons in each experience and move forward with gratitude, compassion and forgiveness for yourself and others. So easy to say, but so hard to do. Bert Ghezzi said it best when he wrote, in *The Angry Christian*, that "resentment is like a poison we carry around inside us with the hope that when we get the chance, we can deposit it where it will harm another who has injured us. The fact is that we carry this poison at extreme risk to ourselves."

If you've ever accidentally touched a hot stovetop, it's human nature to retract your hand. If you've ever been emotionally wounded in a serious relationship, it's human nature to retract your heart. It's not easy to forgive, move forward, or put yourself out there, for fear of being burned again in a relationship, but it's often the way forward to healing and freedom. We forgive not to let the other person off the hook for any wrongdoing, but to release the bitterness within ourselves.

With great compassion, take time to recover and learn from your past experiences. Open your heart to the new opportunities before you again and again and again. It's counterintuitive, but at the right time, forward motion is often part of the healing process whenever there has been an injury in the body. It's the same for the heart.

The Yoga Mindset Formula, Day 4

MOVE

Mountain Pose Alignment Principle #4: Open your Heart

Set your timer for five minutes and move!

The Chest & Back

1. Set your foundation, move the shins forward, pull the thighs back, contract the muscles of your thighs to stand tall. Add that knee-saving micro-bend. Bring the pelvis to neutral and seal the core.
2. Rotate the triceps toward the back. Hug both of the shoulder blades towards the spine and then shift them down slightly. Feel the change in your chest and imagine the heart opening in the process. This motion integrates, stabilizes, and protects the shoulder from injury and allows us to open our chest, contract our shoulder blades and stand taller.

Have you ever noticed that before most people pick up a heavy piece of luggage, they often prepare by grounding the feet about hip width apart, softening the knees, tucking the tailbone under, sealing the core, rotating the triceps towards the back, retracting the shoulder blades back and down and activating the leg muscles to stand tall and integrated? Sound familiar? Yep, you guessed it. It's Mountain Pose. You may have already mastered it if you've ever had to lift a heavy suitcase!

Lifting a heavy object or opening the heart may sound like a no-brainer to most people, but if you stand in a hunched or protective position due to an emotional wound, shifting to a more upright and open position may feel like a journey of a thousand miles. Take it slow. Eventually, in that position, you may start to give and receive love again.

MEDITATE

Set your timer for five minutes. Answer questions three, four, and five, and come back later to answer the other questions, if interested, and as time permits.

1. Can you list the names of one to three people that you've had positive and loving relationships with in the past or the name of someone you are currently in a deeply committed love relationship with at this point in your life?

2. Why do you think it was/is so easy to give and receive love in those relationships?

3. Can you list the names of one to three people that you've had negative love relationships with in the past or the name of someone you are currently in a negative love relationship with at this point in your life?

4. Why do you think it was/is so difficult to give and receive love with them?

5. Can you see any positive results that came from each of the negative love relationships?

6. With those positive lessons in mind, what new stories can you start telling yourself about yourself and the relationships from your past?

7. What changes can you make within yourself to improve the quality of your current or next relationship moving forward? Prioritize the steps, make an action plan and begin to create the relationships and the life you envision for yourself!

MANIFEST

Set your timer for five minutes. Answer question number two and come back later to answer the other questions, if interested, and as time permits. Set your intention for how you will show up in your love relationships, beyond your family of origin, in order to improve the quality of those relationships and to give and receive more love!

1. List the names of one to three people who are easy to love in your life at present, for example, a significant other, a spouse, or your best friend. Ask them how you can love them better or how you can be a better friend. Watch how they respond. Now, this is not meant to be a money game. If someone asks for a million dollars, for example, that may not be realistic or possible for most people, so consider other alternatives. Sometimes, the gift of service, time, or words is much more valuable. Each situation is different. Find out what lights them up. Write the goal next to each person's name and give it a timeline. Cross it off when done.

2. Given the new and empowering stories you choose to tell yourself about your past or present negative love relationships, consider how you can love the difficult people in your life better. Remember that 'showing up' or loving someone doesn't necessarily mean 'in person.' It could be from a distance if being with the other person would be unsafe for you or anyone else involved. Use your best judgment, and then write the goal next to each person's name. It could be as simple and profound as forgiving them as often as needed. Give it some thought, make a plan, and then cross it off when done.

PRACTICE

The Yoga Mindset in REAL TIME

Today, or anytime you feel a desire to open your heart to give and receive more love, take action with the Yoga Mindset in real time.

1. **MOVE:** Stand in Mountain Pose with your shoulders retracted towards the spine and down and heart lifted to the world. Inhale slowly for five to six counts and exhale slowly for five to six counts.
2. **MEDITATE:** Declare that "Life is not happening *to* me, life is happening *for* me."
3. **MANIFEST:** Visualize what you desire in your more serious love relationships and then act on your intention to "show up" in a particular way in those relationships today to improve the relationships and move forward to the best version of yourself and your life.

Yoga Mindset Principle #4:
I have the right to give and receive love.
The Yoga Mindset Mantra:
Life is not happening *to* me, it's happening *for* me.

CHAPTER 5

I Speak

*"It's not about finding your voice,
it's about giving yourself permission
to use your voice."*

Kris Carr

In May of 1990, I said "I do" to the love of my life. Six months later, we were transferred to our first military duty station in Seattle, and a few months after that, he set out on his first six-month deployment to the Middle East for Operation Desert Storm. He was going to war. I was a new bride standing on the dock as the ship pulled away, wondering if he'd be okay, if we'd be okay, if he'd even come home.

Home computers and smartphones were not really a thing yet, so communications were very limited. His occasional calls when in port and hand-written letters kept me afloat. Around mid-deployment, however, things changed significantly. Communication evaporated, and we grew apart. Between the stress of the deployment, distance, lack of communication, and loneliness, we were both casualties of war.

When we were finally reunited, we were together but still miles apart. The tension in the relationship was palpable. I couldn't see a way forward for us. I gave him divorce papers, but he refused to sign them. Instead, we decided to separate while he went on to his next duty station in California. I watched him drive away, and again I wondered if we'd survive.

We both started individual counseling, and that was an eye-opener for me. I was able to work through my own issues, and eventually, I realized that despite everything that had happened, what I really wanted most was not my job, title, position, or salary. It was my soulmate. I would have missed the miracle of living my best life with my best friend and three of the most amazing children in the world, had I not silenced the voices of the world that told me to put self, job, status and financial security above relationships. Speaking up for myself and what I wanted most changed the entire trajectory of my life. The result? The career worked out and, more importantly, so did we. We have let each other down so many more times since then, because we are human, but now, we are committed to working things out quicker and with much more love and grace for each other, for better or for worse.

The Yoga Mindset Formula, Day 5

MOVE

Mountain Pose Alignment Principle #5: Breathe deeply!

Set your timer for five minutes and move!

The Throat, Lungs & Breathwork

1. Set your foundation, shins forward, thighs back, and legs strong. Stand tall and add that knee-saving micro-bend to your knees. Bring your pelvis to neutral and seal the core. Rotate the triceps towards the back. Hug the shoulder blades towards the spine and down, and then open your chest and lift your heart.

2. Holding that position, sweep your arms up over your head as you inhale through your nose for five to six slow counts, pause for five to six counts at the top of your inhale and then sweep your arms down to your sides as you exhale through your nose for five to six slow counts and pause at the bottom of your exhale for five to six counts. If five to six slow counts make you feel a little claustrophobic, try three breaths up and down to start and work towards five breaths at your own pace. Repeat this breath pattern three times.

Have you ever considered how closely the breath is tied to both emotions and the physical body? When you are angry, think about how your body becomes tense and your breath short, irregular, and shallow. Have you noticed it's also a bit harder to talk normally when you are angry?

On the other hand, when you are calm, have you noticed how your body relaxes and your breath becomes long, regular, and deep? As a result of this state of being, your voice is again steady, grounded, and strong. Using our voice to speak words that matter can more easily happen when we are calm and breathing deeply.

In yoga, the goal is to align the breath with the movement for a myriad of reasons. First and foremost, as we synchronize our slow deep breaths with movement, it calms our sympathetic system, also known as the flight or fight response, and it activates the parasympathetic nervous system, also known as the rest and digest response.

"A last word on slow breathing. It goes by another name: prayer." According to James Nestor, the author of the recent eye-opening novel *Breathe*, he states that "when Buddhist monks chant their most popular mantra, each spoken phrase lasts six seconds, with six seconds to inhale before the chant starts again. The Sa Ta Na Ma chant, one of the best-known techniques in Kundalini yoga, also takes six seconds to vocalize, followed by six seconds to inhale. The ancient Hindu khechari each takes six seconds. Japanese, African, Hawaiian, Native American, Buddhist, Taoist, Christian - these cultures and religions all have somehow developed the same prayer techniques, requiring the same breathing patterns. Patricia Gerbarg, MD, and Richard P. Brown, MD would write books and publish several scientific articles about the restorative power of slow breathing, which would become known as "resonant breathing." In many ways, this breathing offered the same benefits as meditation for people who didn't want to meditate. Or yoga, for people who didn't like to get off the couch. It offered the healing touch of prayer for people who weren't religious. Did it matter if we breathed at a rate of six or five seconds or were a half-second off? It did not, as long as the breaths were in the range of 5.5."

"We believe that the rosary may have partly evolved because it synchronized with the inherent cardiovascular (Mayer) rhythms, and this gave a feeling of wellbeing... the Pavia researchers wrote. In other words, the meditations, Ave Marias, and dozens of other prayers that had been developed over the past several thousand years weren't all baseless. Prayer heals, especially when it's practiced at 5.5 breaths a minute." History confirms that slow mindful breathing works.

MEDITATE

Set your timer for five minutes. Choose one or more questions to answer. Come back later to finish the other questions, if interested, and as time permits.

1. Is it difficult for you to speak up for yourself, to verbally state your needs, or to define your boundaries in relationships as a result? Can you list a few examples of situations that are difficult for you verbally? Why do you think they are so difficult?

2. Can you think of one to three negative experiences in your life when your voice was suppressed by yourself or others?

3. Do those negative experiences still affect you negatively today? In what ways?

4. Can you flip the script on those negative thoughts and find any positive results that have come from those one to three negative experiences listed in question number two?

5. What are the things you are most passionate about in your life, and why? Honesty? Integrity? Faith? Literacy? Politics? Mental health issues? Marriage? Family? Health & wellness? The right to life? Equality? Feeding the poor? Helping widows and orphans? Other? Why?

6. Do you believe that you have the right to speak up for yourself and to be heard regarding your needs and the issues that are important to you? Why or why not?

7. What steps do you think you need to take to give yourself permission to use your voice for yourself or others? Make a plan and take action!

MANIFEST

Set your timer for five minutes. Decide how you can show up differently in order to start exercising your right to speak and be heard!

1. Make a list of any difficult discussions or situations you may be facing currently or soon. Consider writing out what the issues are, and consider, step by step, what you will say to that person or to that group. If it's a presentation or meeting, practice making your points in advance with yourself or a trusted friend or family member. If it's a confrontation, honestly review the facts, and identify any part, great or small, that you may have played in the issue. Emotions will be high during a difficult conversation, so just expect it, and remember to breathe slowly to stay calm and use your voice for good. Avoid rabbit trail discussions and focus on the main issue or issues, its effect on you or the group, and some proposals for how everyone can move forward so it, ideally, doesn't happen again. Ensure that both sides have the opportunity to speak and be heard. If that is not possible, a third unbiased party may need to be invited into the discussion as a mediator.

PRACTICE

The Yoga Mindset in REAL TIME:

Today, or anytime, when you feel a desire to really listen to someone, or to speak and be heard, especially where it is related to your needs, or any issues that matter to you, take action with the Yoga Mindset in real time!

1. **MOVE:** Inhale slowly for five to six counts and exhale slowly for five to six counts and stand in Mountain Pose with your chin lifted. Take a deep breath and give yourself permission to use your voice. Remember that you have the right to speak and be heard.

2. **MEDITATE:** Declare that "Life is not happening *to* me, life is happening *for* me."

3. **MANIFEST:** Visualize yourself not only finding your voice but also giving yourself permission to use it when it matters. When negative thoughts arise, making it hard to speak up, catch yourself. Remind yourself that you have the right to speak and be heard. Consider how you will 'show up' differently in your life and the lives of others as a result of that realization and the new positive stories that you are telling yourself about your voice, and then take action. Dig deep for the courage and speak up in a class, a meeting, a discussion, a debate, or a presentation. You have a voice and a story. Share it to lift others up.

Yoga Mindset Principle #5:
I have the right to speak and be heard.
The Yoga Mindset Mantra:
"Life is not happening *to* me, it's happening *for* me.

CHAPTER 6

I See

"I was blind,
but now
I see."

John 9:25, The NIV Bible

On October 31, 2016, after four years of living and working abroad in Singapore, our family was transferred back to the United States. Trust me when I say that it was more 'trick' than 'treat' to return to the US on that particular Halloween.

While we were living overseas, our eldest son was at college studying Architecture, and Thanksgiving break was just around the corner. I couldn't wait to see him again. During Middle School, he had been diagnosed with High Functioning Aspergers or High-Functioning Autism, as it's now called, but he had made it through both high school and college with minimal support. Physically and intellectually, he had no issues at all. Soft social and communication skills were another thing altogether, however.

Approximately two weeks after our return to Virginia, he ended up in the ER near his college due to a breakdown that no one, including my son, can explain still to this day. After riding that family crisis rollercoaster for the first twenty-four hours, I was able to recover my balance by choosing my focal point and steadily fixing my gaze on a future that included a new level of healing.

Based on watching my mom over the years, I had a feeling it would also get worse before it got better, and that's exactly what happened. Having seen my mother struggle with mental health issues was, oddly, the perfect preparation. Even that had been working for me all along I realized. That thought helped me to quickly switch from asking why him, why me, why us, to knowing, deep in my soul, that we'd all get through it together with a lot of love and support. I knew it would take time, but in faith, before I had hindsight or proof of healing, trusting that life was working for me, I spoke healing into the universe, and I watched and waited for the miracle.

After three gut-wrenching years, we survived to see the miracle of his stabilization, thanks to God, prayer, doctors, medication, and unconditional love. My eyes were opened to the mental health issues all around me, hidden in plain sight. I had been blind, but now I could see both my mom, my son and so many others, so much more clearly.

The Yoga Mindset Formula, Day 6

MOVE

Set your timer for five minutes and move!

Mountain Pose Alignment Principle #6: Fix your gaze!

The Eyes

1. Set your foundation. Shins forward, thighs back, legs strong, and standing tall. Add that knee-saving micro-bend, bring the pelvis to neutral, seal the core, rotate the triceps towards the back. Hug the shoulder blades towards the spine and down. Open your chest and lift your heart.

2. Next, lift your gaze to look straight ahead. Pull the jawline back slightly so that the head is stacked squarely over the neck and spine. Find your focal point, about three feet, or a meter, in front of you. It can be anything, but it should be something that is not moving. Fix your eyes softly on that spot and begin your breathwork. Inhale for five to six slow breaths and then exhale for five to six slow breaths. Repeat one to three times.

In the same way that you found and fixed your gaze on a point in the distance during your breathwork, consider how that concept applies to your life. What is the focal point of your life right now? Is your gaze in life fixed on the most important thing to help you reach the best version of yourself and the best version of your life as you envision it? If not, what changes do you need to make to find your new focal point?

MEDITATE

Set your timer for five minutes. Answer question number three below. Come back later to answer the other questions, if interested, and as time permits.

Did you know that, initially, yoga was more about the ability to quiet the mind than the yoga poses? Some people refer to the practice of quieting the mind and focusing on something as meditation. Others refer to it as prayer. Whatever you call it, it's been practiced and documented for thousands of years. Meditation sounds easy, but can be quite challenging because we all get stuck in the past, and the future, in our minds, so easily and so often. It's hard to stay present. How many times have you said, "Ugh, I should have done this or said that," or "I know that this meeting is not going to go well, or I know that something bad is going to happen." The mind spins wildly between the past and the future, which is exhausting, but there is a way to reel the mind back into the present. Through the practice of focused meditation, or prayer, we can start to pull the mind back into the present and start living with increased peace and calm and decreased stress and overwhelm. It's not easy to quiet the monkey mind swinging to and fro, but like everything else, practice makes progress.

As you practice meditating, keep coming back to your focal point, to your breath, to your heartbeat, to the way your body feels in Mountain Pose, or to your anchoring thought or intention for the day. The mind will wander. When it does, just smile, knowing this is what the mind does best, and then come back to the focal point, the anchor, and the breath. That is success in meditation or prayer.

Just like lifting weights, meditating or praying, is both a practice and a process. Be kind and be patient with yourself. The more we lift weights, the stronger we get, but it takes time. The more we pray and meditate, the more we can focus and stay present, but it takes time. Consistency is key.

1. Do you feel like you are someone who really sees others, including those closest to you, possibly hiding serious struggles while in plain sight? If not, why not, and what steps can you take to become more aware and supportive of your friends and family?

2. Do you feel like you are someone who allows themselves to be seen, or do you tend to hide your true self? If so, why and what steps can you take to become more transparent and authentically yourself with your closest family and friends?

3. What is the main focal point of your life, and is that helping you to live a balanced and successful life? Why or why not? Does it need to shift to a new focal point?

MANIFEST

Set your timer for five minutes. Answer question number one below. Come back later to answer the other questions, if interested, and as time permits. Flip the script on seeing and being seen with your family and friends.

1. If appropriate, and only if no harm will come to you or anyone else in the process, identify one thing that you'd like to share with someone that you trust, maybe a family member or a close friend, in order to build a stronger relationship, or in order to become the most authentic version of yourself both inside and out.

2. If appropriate, and only if no harm will come to you or anyone else in the process, identify one person in your family, or perhaps a close friend, who you think, or know, may have a lot going on in their lives right now. Consider how you can reach out to them in order to see how they are actually doing. Some will welcome the concern and care, but others may not. That's okay. Everyone is on their own journey. For those that welcome your kindness, consider asking, "How can I help?" and watch how that offer affects them, and then to the best of your ability, do what you can do to better support them.

PRACTICE

The Yoga Mindset in REAL TIME:

Today, or anytime you want to see and be seen more clearly in your relationships, take action with the Yoga Mindset in real time!

1. **MOVE:** Inhale slowly for five to six counts and exhale slowly for five to six counts and stand in Mountain Pose. Lift your gaze and softly fix your gaze on the person, or the issue, in front of you, remembering that you have the choice to see and be seen.
2. **MEDITATE:** Declare that "Life is not happening *to* me, life is happening *for* me."
3. **MANIFEST:** Visualize yourself seeing, really seeing others, as they are, and then visualize yourself as being clearly seen. What would that look like in your life? Who can you trust? Give yourself permission to observe your emotions and the emotions of others, their facial expressions, their body language, their energy, and a myriad of other unspoken factors you can 'see' in your relationships if interested in really looking closely.

Yoga Mindset Principle #6:
I have the ability to see and be seen.
The Yoga Mindset Mantra:
"Life is not happening *to* me, life is happening *for* me."

CHAPTER 7

I Know

"You are a child of God...
...meant to shine, as children do.
...born to make manifest the glory of God..."

Marianne Williamson

My paternal great-grandfather immigrated to southwest Pennsylvania from Bohemia around 1870. He and his German wife had eleven children who worked the farm and mostly lived through the roaring 20s, the Great Depression, World War I, World War II, the Korean War, and the Vietnam War. Two of their children, my two favorite great-aunts, had a genuine love for life, God, country, and others. They walked with God daily in a vibrant and abiding relationship that seemed to give meaning, purpose, and a shine to everything that they did. They loved and served God by loving and serving others through the selfless giving of their time and talents. They volunteered, taught children's church, cared for the poor, visited the sick in hospitals, and weekly visited and decorated the graves of deceased family members with bouquets of flowers from their garden. They were the salt of the earth, and their goodness flowed deeply into my soul when I visited every summer from the age of nine to twenty-nine.

It was their constant desire and joy to remind me that God created me, delighted in me, and loved me more than anything in the whole world. As a small child, they introduced me to the concept of God in nature on their hundred-acre farm. On every nature walk, they helped me see God in every acorn, every giant oak tree, every dandelion, and every firefly filling up the dark summer night sky from the swing on the porch of their farmhouse. Church occurred daily in their massive garden. God was in every seed that was planted, every tender shoot that would sprout, and every leaf and blossom that would unfurl to the sun and the rain.

As a child, it was all magic, adventure, and fantastic stories with my aunts and little sister in the garden, but little did I know they were introducing me to the importance of staying connected and communing with God, the ultimate power source and the Creator of everything. I accepted that invitation as a young child, and hold out that invitation to you, too. Elevate your mind daily and commune with God to co-create the best version of your life together!

If you are really interested in moving forward in your life, no matter what circumstance you are in, and you feel like you've tried it all and nothing has worked, why not try plugging in, or back in, to a limitless power source, the Creator of the Universe. Consider connecting daily, as you would with a dear friend, by meeting, talking, and listening to one another in a relationship. Then, watch for the seemingly random and small things that may start to happen as confirmation in your life and as a result of connecting to the Divine.

I can really only speak from the point of view of a Christian on the topic of starting a relationship with God, so if you are open to learning more about how to meditate within the Christian faith, consider this ancient Christian meditation practice called Lectio Divina, which is Latin for 'divine reading'. Don't have a bible? No worries. There is an app for that! If possible, download The Bible App. Alternatively, you could just search any book of the bible online. If technology is not your thing, then try a recycled bookstore. The NIV or ESV version is easy to read. Whatever you select, just make sure you can understand it. If you get to a passage that is hard to understand, use technology for a detailed explanation. Start with the Book of Mark, the Psalms or Proverbs, as a text to meditate on daily. If not the Bible, then any other inspirational book will do. Perhaps a favorite book of poetry or prose. Or possibly a novel or any other inspirational book. Whatever you decide to read, there are five steps to the process of divine reading, and freelance writer Elizabeth Menneh laid them out beautifully:

Lectio Divina (Divine Reading for a Daily Meditation Practice)

- **Prepare**

    I'd suggest 30 minutes to read, reflect, and respond to the Holy Spirit's promptings in Lectio Divina. To tune in, I like to light a candle, not because it's necessary, but because the flame and fragrance serve as gentle reminders when collecting my thoughts and calming my mind. I pray a prayer of invitation, saying something like, "God, let me hear from you," and spend a few moments sitting quietly so my mind is open to hearing from God.

- **Read (Lectio)**

    My first reading is an opportunity to get to know the Scripture passage. I listen carefully for any words or phrases that seem to jump out. It's important not to force things but wait patiently for God to give gentle guidance. One day when reading Jeremiah 31, I felt my mind drawn to the strength of God's commitment to His covenant: "[I will make a new covenant] not like the covenant that I made with their fathers on the day when I took them by the hand to bring them out of the land of Egypt, my covenant that they broke, though I was their husband." (Jeremiah 31:32 English Standard Version. I was struck by the image of God leading His people by the hand as an act of love – they weren't left to begin their momentous journey alone.

- **Reflect(Meditatio)**

  The second reading of the same passage focuses further on the points I become aware of during the first reading. Often I'll just re-read a few verses so I can reflect carefully on where God had nudged me. Then I'll reflect on what I believe God is saying, I try not to analyze the passage. It's easy to slip into "study mode" and think about interesting points rather than listening to what God might be saying. It helps to ask God to make his focus clear.

- **Respond (Oratio)**

  After a third reading, it's time to respond. I like to record my thoughts by journaling because I know I'm very prone to forgetting what I've learned, even by the next day! We can respond in prayer too, which gives us the opportunity for a conversation with God. When reading Jeremiah, I journaled my wonderings. If God is so powerfully committed to keeping His covenant with me, why do I sometimes lack the commitment to stay close to God? Often the events of the day crowd in, and I don't always make time to listen to God. I prayed that God would help me to prioritize spending time with Him.

- **Rest (Contemplatio)**

  After the final reading, I spent around 10 minutes in silent contemplation… I just sit quietly and allow God to work. When my mind starts to wander and dart here and there, I bring it gently back to stillness again… It's important to remember that Lectio Divina is not an end in itself or another spiritual practice to tick off our to-do list. It helps us hear specifically and individually for God through Scripture, guided by the Holy Spirit, and deepens our relationship with Him.

As you grow deeper in a relationship with God, divine love will flow into your life and it can help to empower you to better love and serve others. To get that close, though, you have to believe that you are welcome into that relationship. My dear reader, without a doubt, you are. No matter what you've done or who you are, all are welcome. Come as you are.

The Yoga Mindset Formula, Day 7

MOVE

Mountain Pose Alignment Principle #7: Lift the crown of your head!

Set your timer for 5 minutes and move!

The Head

1. Set the foundation by moving feet hip-width apart and toes forward. Move the shins forward, thighs back, keep the legs strong, and stand tall. Add that knee-saving micro-bend, bring the pelvis to a neutral position, seal the core, rotate the triceps towards the back and the palms forward slightly. Hug the shoulder blades towards the spine and down, open your chest and lift your heart. Lift your gaze to look straight ahead, with the jawline pulled back, ears over shoulders, and head in line with the spine, find a focal point about a meter or more in front of you. Fix your eyes softly on that spot. Inhale for five to six slow counts as you sweep your arms up over your head, pause for five to six slow counts at the top of your inhale, then sweep your arms down to your sides as you exhale for five to six slow counts and pause at the bottom of your exhale for five to six counts.

2. As you inhale and exhale, focus on lifting the head up a little higher, and as you do, consider your relationship with the Creator of the Universe. The Creator knows you and desires to

be in a relationship with you. You can tap into the power of the Divine by simply speaking to God as you would another person. Imagine God as a good and loving parent who wants only the best for you. Let that unconditional love flow into you, healing and empowering you to love others supernaturally as you move through your day today.

MEDITATE

Set your timer for five minutes, and answer questions seven and eight. Come back later to answer the other questions, if interested, and as time permits.

1. Has your experience with God or religion been positive, negative, or neutral? Why?

2. Do you believe in God, or some version of a God, or a Creator of everything?

3. Do you believe that God wants to know you intimately? Why or why not?

4. Do you tend to keep communication one way, or do you try to listen for the quiet voice of God, too? Why or why not?

5. Does the thought of an intimate relationship with God cause some fear within you? Why or why not?

6. What is one thing you can do today to deepen your connection with the Creator of everything?

7. Can you list one to three negative experiences you've had in a relationship with God? What happened?

8. Can you write out a positive result that may have resulted from each of those negative experiences?

MANIFEST

Set your timer for five more minutes. Answer question number two. Come back later to answer question number one, if interested, and as time permits.

1. Consider the concept of the Creator of everything. Then imagine that Creator as the most perfect parent who loves you unconditionally and desires to be in a relationship with you. Can you receive that love? Why or why not?

2. Imagine yourself as free from fear and judgment by God and consider how that could change the way you "show up" in relationship with the Infinite Creator of the Universe.

PRACTICE

The Yoga Mindset in REAL TIME

Today, or anytime you desire to grow deeper in relationship with the Creator, take action with the Yoga Mindset in real time.

1. **MOVE:** Inhale slowly for five to six counts and then exhale slowly for five to six counts while standing in Mountain Pose. Lift the top of your head up towards the heavens, remembering that you have the right to know and be known by God.

2. **MEDITATE:** Declare that "Life is not happening *to* me, life is happening *for* me."

3. **MANIFEST:** Visualize yourself in an intimate relationship with God, the Creator of everything. What would that look like in your life? What steps can you take to make that a reality daily?

Yoga Mindset Principle #7:
I have the right to know and be known.
The Yoga Mindset Mantra:
"Life is not happening *to* me, life is happening *for* me.

CHAPTER 8

We Are

"One day
when I was sitting quiet...
it came to me:
that feeling of being part of everything,
not separate at all..."

The Color Purple, by Alice Walker

Congratulations! You made it to the top of the mountain!

How's the view? Hopefully, it is spectacular and possibly, life-altering. Can you also look down to the base of your personal mountain journey and 'see' all the stops that you made along the path? Can you see the various fragments of your life at each stop? Can you see how those fragments all fit together with lines of gold, telling their stories? Can you look over all of it, seeing the light of the sun reflecting off of the lines of gold, and like the Samurai warrior in the opening story of this book, say that you are pleased? If so, you have truly reached the summit of this mountain. If not, don't despair. Some areas of our lives take more time to work through. Go back to the area of your life where you may still feel stuck. Do the work of journaling and the Yoga Mindset Formula daily, possibly professional help, until you breakthrough. You may be closer than you think to your personal breakthrough.

If this journey was beneficial for you, good news: there is more! Now, you can move forward, as you are, perfectly imperfect, with all the fragments of your life on display in lines of gold telling their story for all to see. Your confidence to be your real self and to speak about those life experiences may start to help others come out of hiding and give you access into the struggles of their lives, too. That will be your opportunity to be courageous and share your story about how you weathered the storm and flipped the script to move forward to your best self and your best life. It will be your opportunity to speak hope into the seemingly impossible and to guide them on a journey up their personal mountain, too.

You have a role to play. You were born for a reason and a purpose, and everything you have experienced, or are currently experiencing, has all been working together for you. If you are in the middle of a storm, it will be hard to see it. That is when faith and your mindset step in. Trust that the Creator of everything does His best work in the dark. Look for the lessons, reach out for help, and move forward as quickly as possible so you can get back to fulfilling your purpose in this life.

You have work to do in the short amount of time you've been given on this earth. As Albert Schwitzer said, "I don't know what your destiny will be, but one thing I know: The only ones among you who will really be happy are those who have sought and found how to serve."

There are so many other people in the world who need to know that they are not alone in whatever battle they are facing. We are all kintsugi, and we are all connected, and the journey up and down the mountain never actually ends for any of us. We are all just at different points on the mountain at different times in our lives. We'll continue to go up and down the mountain, and in and out of the alignment principles, to constantly adjust and readjust, or connect another fragment of our life to our story over the course of our entire lives.

The storms of life will continue to slam into you. On that, you can depend, but now you can also depend on the Yoga Mindset to help you change the direction of your sail, harness the gale-force winds to carry you to your chosen destination. Storms can be devastating, but it's not actually the storm that breaks you. It's never been about the storm. It's always been about your mindset, your response, and the story you tell yourself every day afterward that either traps you in the past or frees you to move forward to a better future. Will you respond in fear or faith? Keep the Yoga Mindset with you wherever you go. When the next storm comes, before you respond, remember:

MOVE: Inhale for five to six slow counts and exhale for five to six slow counts. Repeat one to three times, and stand grounded, integrated, and resilient in Mountain Pose.

MEDITATE: Declare to yourself, "Life is not happening *to* me, life is happening *for* me." Look for the positive lessons in every situation and create a new, better, and empowering story.

MANIFEST: Visualize the life you want, rewire your mind to create a better future for yourself and let the words of your vision echo softly into the universe. Make a plan and take action. Free yourself to move forward towards the best version of yourself and your life as you define it by sharing your story and lifting others up.

Change your mindset, change your life!

You are the author of your life story, but it may not happen the way you envision it if you don't write the script. You have the power to dream and imagine and reach out for help and support to get there. It all starts with a breath, a thought, and then an action. It starts with moving, meditating, and manifesting. It starts with the Yoga Mindset.

Choose how you will show up for your life from this day forward. Learn the lessons of the cracks in your life. Mend them with precious lines of gold and start living your life to the fullest as a perfectly imperfect vessel.

Let your life be a spectacular skyscraper firmly anchored into a massive, level, and stable foundation deep beneath the earth. See your life soaring to the heavens in communion with the Divine, love itself, as your ultimate power source. Make your life a masterpiece. Let it inspire others. Let it be a breathtaking mosaic life, telling its story in lines of gold.

It will take great courage to display and talk about those lines of gold in your life, but it is the very thing that can free you up and propel you forward to the best version of yourself and your life. There is great power in your story. Embrace it. Celebrate it. Share it. Use it to lift others up. You have a purpose to fulfill in the very short amount of time you've been given. There is nothing more important.

NEXT STEPS!

Now that you have had a small taste of the power of changing your life through The Yoga Mindset, keep going! Prioritize your health, take care of your body, go deeper into the seven alignment secrets, learn how to apply those alignment principles not only to every other yoga pose you hope to master, but also your life on a daily basis. Move, meditate and manifest the best version of yourself and your life in real time with me in a FREE 3-Day Yoga Mindset Group Challenge. To join this challenge, click here:
http://www.mosaicconcepts.com/yogachallenge

The FREE 3 Day Yoga Mindset Challenge includes:
- 3 - 15 minute Yoga Mindset Formula Sessions
- 3 - Yoga Sessions
- 3 - Movement, Meditation & Manifestation Sessions

Alternatively, if you want to bypass the Challenge, you have more options. I'm also offering an 8, 10 and 12 Week Online Yoga Mindset Certification Course and a 9 month Yoga Teacher Training (1 weekend intensive per month online). If you have any questions about these additional options, or you are ready to sign up for one of this additional options, schedule a FREE 1 on 1 consultation call with me, or my team, here:
https://calendly.com/mosaicconcepts-coachmichelle

THE YOGA MINDSET

Take the next step. Make The Yoga Mindset a way of life. Ground yourself in this 15 minute daily mindfulness practice, so that you can rise up, reach out and move forward in your life with passion, power and purpose. Connect with The Yoga Mindset tribe. Come together as the spectacular mosaic of people that you are, from all around the world to move, meditate and manifest the best version of yourself and your life as you envision it together.

Thank you so much for practicing extravagant self-care by joining me on this journey through The Yoga Mindset. I hope that it was all that you hoped for, that you made it to the top of your epic mountain of a life (or are at least getting closer to the summit) and that the view was life-changing for you, too.

Remember, it's a lifetime journey of going up and down that mountain and revising your intentions for your life. Remember that moment when you caught a glimpse of that view of your best self and your best life. Set aside 15 minutes every day and reconnect with yourself and that vision every morning with The Yoga Mindset Formula. Experience that vision for your life with all your senses and then do the work of making your dreams a reality by taking action. Harness the force of the storms of life to your advantage and your chosen destination. Look for the ways life is working for you and then celebrate them. Keep flipping the script on those storms of life and the stories you tell yourself about them. It's all in how you look at it. Change your mindset, change your life.

As the author of your life story, the pen is always in your hand. You get to choose your life story. What new stories will you write? Another way to think about it is to ask yourself what you'd want people to say about you at your funeral or in a memorial article. Now, that changes things up a bit, doesn't it? Time is short, my dear reader. Make the most of it. Make your life a masterpiece. The sky's the limit and that means the options are infinite!

As you continue your personal journey through this crazy amazing world, my wish for you is a loving-kindness meditation that my yoga mentors often speak over me and their other yoga students at the end of a practice. Read it out loud three times, slowly, and let it sink into your heart, soul and mind: May you be safe, may you be healthy, may you be happy and may you walk through the world with ease. Namaste.

Change your mindset, change your life!

DOWNLOAD YOUR FREE GIFTS

Read This First

Just to say thanks for buying and reading my journal, I would like to give you three bonus gifts for FREE, no strings attached!

To Download Now, Visit:
www.TheYogaMindsetJournal.com/JournalFreeGifts

I appreciate your interest in my book, and I value your feedback as it helps me improve future versions of this book. I would appreciate it if you could leave your invaluable review on Amazon.com with your feedback. Thank you!

References

Carr, Kris, *"It's not about finding your voice…,"* https://kriscarr.com/

Carrey, Jim, (November 2017), *"Life doesn't happen to you, it happens for you,"* Retrieved from YouTube Full Speech: Jim Carrey's Commencement Address at the Maharishi International University @ https://www.youtube.com/watch?v=koLqxXcuq3s

Catron, Mandy Len, (2015, August), *Falling in Love is the Easy Part,* https://www.ted.com/talks/mandy_len_catron_falling_in_love_is_the_easy_part

Chapman, Gary, *The 5 Love Languages,* Northfield Publishing, 2010

Chopra, Deepak, *The Path to Love,* Harmony Books, 1997

Cloud, Henry Dr., *9 Things You Simply Must Do,* Integrity Publishers, 2004

Cushnir, Raphael, *Setting Your Heart on Fire,* Broadway Books, 2003

Davis, Pam, *Kintsugi: The Value of a Broken Bowl,* The Younique Foundation

Dickens, Charles, *A Tale of Two Cities,* Ino Editions, 2018

Downing, Jim, *Meditation,* NavPress, 2011

Farris, Jon Val, *"From Broken to Beautiful: The Power of Kintsugi,"* HuffPost Contributor Platform, December 2017

Gates, Rolf, *Meditations on Intention and Being*, Anchor Books, December 2015

Gawain, Shakti, *Creative Visualization*, Nataraj Publishing, 2002

Hensel, Gary, *I Am*, Balboa Printing, December 2016

Hood, Katie (2019, June), *The Difference Between Healthy and Unhealthy Love*, Retrieved from Ted Talks at https://www.youtube.com/watch?v=ON4iy8hq2hM

Jacobsen, Wayne, *The Vineyard*, Harvest House, 1992

Judith, Anodea, *Chakra Balancing*, Sounds True Publishing, 2003

Leatherbury, Hannah, *5 Yoga Practices to Balance the Throat Chakra*, Retrieved at yogiapproved.com at https://www.yogiapproved.com/om/throat-chakra-healing-yoga-practices/

Lindberg, Anne Morrow, *Gift of the Sea*, Pantheon Publishing, 1991

MacDonald, Gordon, *Ordering Your Private World*, Thomas Nelson Publishing, 1985

Menneh, Elizabeth (2020 March), *Lectio Divina: A Beginner's Guide*, Retrieved from Busted Halo, https://bustedhalo.com/ministry-resources/lectio-divina-beginners-guide

Moore, Catherine, *Positive Daily Affirmations: Is There Science Behind It?*, Retrieved from PositivePsychology.com at https://positivepsychology.com/daily-affirmations/

Myers, Thomas W., *Anatomy Trains*, Churchill Livingstone, February 2014

Myss, Caroline, *Anatomy of the Spirit*, Three Rivers Press, 1996

Neruda, Pablo, *Love Sonnet XI*, Retrieved from PoetryAnalysis.com at https://www.pablonerudapoems.com/sonnet-xi/

Nestor, James, *Breathe*, Riverhead Books, 2020

Robbins, Mel, *The Five Second Rule*, Savio Republic Publishing, 2017

Ruiz, Don Miguel, *The Four Agreements*, Amber-Allen Publishing, 1997

Schwitzer, Albert, *"I don't know what your destiny will be…,"* Goodreads

Sinek, Simon, *What's the Best Way to Confront Someone*, Retrieved from YouTube Video at https://www.youtube.com/watch?v=dCkxgICCVWU

Smith, James Bryan, *Embracing the Love of God*, Harper Collins San Francisco

Smith, Kathy, *How to Actually Practice Mountain Pose – There's More Technique Than You Think*, www.yogiapproved.com,

Thich, Nhat Hanh, *Please Call Me by My True Names,* Retrieved plumvillage.org at https://plumvillage.org/articles/please-call-me-by-my-true-names-song-poem/

Walker, Alice, *The Color Purple*, Pocket Publishing, March 1987

Williamson, Marianne, *Our Deepest Fear*, 1996, https://poemanalysis.com/marianne-williamson/our-deepest-fear/

Yax, John & Chris, Yax Yoga Concepts and The Complete Posture Blueprint, www.yaxyogaconcepts.com

Acknowledgments

I had no idea how many people it takes to create a book! There is no way to acknowledge them all, but I'd like to give credit to a few…

To the first, best, and most creative author, who, with just a breath, spoke everything in this magical and mysterious universe into being. It is a delight to know and walk closely with you.

To Cris Cawley, CEO of Game Changer Publishing, and her amazing Publishing Crew, thank you for your outstanding wisdom and guidance on every detail from the thousand foot viewpoint.

To Ms. Alyea, my ninth grade English Teacher, thank you for noticing my first efforts at writing and for sparking the flame for language arts deep inside of me.

To the Yax Yoga Brothers, John and Chris, thank you for teaching from the heart, for the gift of your knowledge and for de-mystifying yoga just enough so that it was finally and fully accessible and then re-mystifying just enough so that it remained fully magic and intoxicating mystery.

To all the inspirational authors, and their books decorating so many of the walls and corners of my home, thank you, thank you, thank you for sucking the marrow out of life so that we might live: Maya Angelou's *I Know Why the Caged Bird Sings*, Jane Austen's *Pride and Prejudice*, Corrie Ten Boom's *The Hiding Place*, Geraldine Brooks'

Year of Wonder and *March*, Elizabeth Barrett Browning's *Selected Poems*, Pat Conroy's *Beach Music*, Charles Dickens' *A Tale of Two Cities*, Kristen Hannah's *The Nightingale*, O. Henry's *The Gift of the Magi*, James Hilton's *Lost Horizon*, C.S. Lewis' *The Lion, The Witch and The Wardrobe*, Anne Morrow Lindbergh's *The Gift of the Sea*, John Steinbeck's *The Grapes of Wrath*, J.R.R. Tolkien's *Lord of the Rings Trilogy*, to name a few.

To my parents, you made it, we made it. Thank you for celebrating the lines of gold in your life in the hopes that it might help even just one person.

To my brilliant husband, Dan, thank you for being an eternal optimist and for always reminding me how to eat the elephant of a book - one bite at a time. Organization really is your superpower!

Last but not least, to my three wonderful children, thank you for going solo for months when I was MIA while writing this book. #mykidsareadulting! I love you, I love you more...INFINITY!

www.ingramcontent.com/pod-product-compliance
Lightning Source LLC
Chambersburg PA
CBHW061147040426
42445CB00013B/1592